This book is not about organizing your closet or deep cleaning your house within an inch of its life.

Dixie Lee Johnson

I Can't Clean, Don't Make Me!

The Lazy Way to Conquer the Mess

Dixie Lee Johnson

Illustrated by Surbhi Pitti

I Can't Clean, Don't Make Me!
The Lazy Way to Conquer the Mess

Edited by Seb Jenkins   sebjenkins@hotmail.co.uk
Illustrated by Surbhi Pitti   surbhipitti@gmail.com
Layout by Rokit Books   rokitent@gmail.com

Dixie Lee Johnson
Visit my website at *www.dixieleejohnson.com*

Printed in the United States of America

First Printing
ISBN-9781790133512

Published by Rokit Books

Dedications

I would like to dedicate this book to my husband Rick who participated in countless edits and rewrites of this manuscript supporting me all the way.

Also to my brother Rick who brought all the technical aspects together that I would never have been able to complete on my own.

And to my sister Janny, who helped me at a point when I was hopelessly stuck. To my other sisters Geri Lyn and Beki and to my parents, all of whom provided the experiences of their lives to frame this text.

Most importantly, I want to dedicate these writings to the stars of the story, my sons David and Jeff who precipitated the journaling of the events of this book.

I would also like to extend my gratitude to my very talented illustrator, Surbhi Pitti who produced the sketches that helped bring the manuscript to life.

Lastly my editor, Seb Jenkins, who did a wonderful job perfecting every line, every concept and bringing forth an ideal conclusion to this book.

Table of Contents

Introduction
I Can't Clean,
Don't Make Me!

DO YOU THROW ALL your energy in your day job and then collapse when you get home while the mess continues to accumulate around you? Do you have dirty dishes left in the sink for days? Is it past time to empty the cat box? Are you afraid people might drop by because your house is unsightly? Do you really hate the mess but are too overwhelmed to get a handle on it? Do you feel paralyzed by your situation? Do you wait for your mother-in-law's visit then clean the house in a panic? Do you have to "pre-clean" before you can hire a cleaning service? If you answer yes to at least three of these questions then this is the book for you.

Most of us know how to clean but for many reasons can't find the time or motivation to do it. Some folks try to justify their situation and say, "Messy doesn't bother me."

That may be true for moderately messy homes, perhaps a little cluttered. But that's not what this is about. I'm talking about major *Messer-uppers*.

Some of us are born lazy, or are weak due to health reasons, or are battling psychological issues. There are a thousand reasons that people have the "really messy house syndrome." These people hide in their homes miserable in their situation. I found a paltry few books or articles that address this segment of the population. Most books on the subject of "cleaning your home" turn out to be elaborate schemes to organize, beautify your home or promote feng shui. They promise simple methods yet I found most of them to be dizzyingly complicated for myself or readers for whom I am writing this book. We aren't there yet, are we?

This book is not for the hoarder. That takes a team of professionals and a psychologist at the least. I'm dedicating

I CAN'T CLEAN, DON'T MAKE ME!

this writing to people who aren't afraid to throw things away and need a little direction. This book is not about organizing your closet or garage or deep cleaning your house within an inch of its life. All that comes later. This book is about starting to inch forward in new ways that has had little attention in the genre of self-help "cleaning" books. I am simply putting forth a plan for folks who want to get on top of the problem with the least effort.

Growing up in a large family we were well off enough that our parents hired a maid 5 days week, 8 hours a day to pick up after our messy selves. We didn't make our beds, we threw our clothes on the floor and left the dishes for the maid the next morning. Mom taught us how to clean, wash clothes and do dishes etc. but we lacked the will to do it. Any chore assigned to us was met with disdain and resistance.

The methods I'm proposing is for the individual who is too overwhelmed, overworked and overcome that when they return from a hard day or night at work have to face preparing a meal and cleaning up. Maybe some us are just plain lazy, or have good reason to be, so we muddle through it, leave the dishes and plop on the couch in front of the TV until bed time. All the while the mess is building up around us.

The following chapters discuss ways to break down the intimidating task an inch at a time. I want to put forth a manageable way to conquer the impossible.

The first chapter deals with children and helping them to get control of their own space. The title "Start Early" will help you to recognize some patterns in your own past that may have contributed to how you got to where you are today. It also speaks to parents of toddlers and children and offers some solutions. The rest of the book centers on the adult and their domain which is the rest of the home. I discuss ways to prepare yourself for a journey into tidiness with extra tips along the way to help maintain your progress. Moving from one room to another, I describe uncomplicated steps for improvement. Also, I include some true stories of my family and my short comings that may seem inconceivable to some folks yet some with which you might actually identify. Lastly, I review some of the strong points to remember and add a few more hints for good measure.

I CAN'T CLEAN, DON'T MAKE ME!

Reading this book will definitely impact your life in ways you never before thought. Everyone most assuredly will walk away with a new perspective on the way they view what was once thought to be a mountain to conquer. House cleaning will appear as little hills to climb.

Join me on this journey to a simpler life.

Chapter 1
Start Early

MESSY HOUSE, MESSY LIFE!

After an exhausting day of work, I slogged home, opened the front door and spotted my two teens sitting on the floor surrounded by filth and foul, playing video games.

The room was littered with potato chips, coke cans, books and papers on the couch, coats thrown over chairs, shoes and socks tossed randomly. I spied a cigarette butt on a plate on the coffee table and some keys soon to fall between the couch cushions. As my head spun around three times and I was about to spew green stuff, they fled a split second later

I CAN'T CLEAN, DON'T MAKE ME!

with fear in their eyes. They dropped everything and flew out the back leaving the door swinging on its hinges. My two boys were avoiding the screaming and ranting of an insane woman at her tipping point. Both would return later after the demon was gone.

I succumbed to my gloom, kicked off my shoes, scooped books and papers from the couch and then after rescuing the keys I plopped down amid the quiet chaos. Waiting to calm down I told myself I would deal with those two later. Soon someone would have to clean up this mess then cook dinner. I thought to myself "Cook? Ugh." A few minutes later I surrendered and called for pizza. Once the boys returned they did a half-hearted job picking up random items. We ate pizza and watched TV the rest of the evening.

Overcome by what I saw as an enormous task to keep my house presentable I would occasionally ask one of my siblings or my mom for help but it wasn't long before the place would return to a state of disorder. I was too broke to hire a steady housekeeper. I was a single parent with a very demanding job while studying for advanced certifications after finishing my undergraduate degree, I usually spent my free time entertaining my kids. Then I would return to laziness leaving my house as the last priority. The guilt was always there and I never stopped hoping I could find a way out of the dilemma.

I usually didn't have a clue where to start. Over time I tried to formulate some short cuts. I thought of a way to get the teens to clean their messy room.

I safety-pinned the top sheet to the comforter of the bed so they would merely have to pull the covers up in the morning.

I placed a laundry basket at the foot of each bed providing an easy toss for dirty clothes.

A small trash receptacle was put near each laundry basket for random discards.

Complimenting myself on such a brilliant idea I went to check their room a few days later. I was shocked to see that the only clean areas in the room were the laundry baskets and the trash cans. The covers were still pinned to the sheets but they were balled up at the foot of each bed.

With a deep sense of failure, I allowed myself to be defeated for some time after that. Now, I won't say that the previous endeavor would not work for some folks but I raised two of the devils' spawn. The message here is, if you have kids it is best to start early. After my two grew up and went into the Navy then married, either the Navy or the wives or both managed to drive home the wisdom of picking up after oneself. Today they are much tidier adults.

Being an observer of the human condition, I majored in Psychology. Although I might have a lazy, messy spirit I have an intensive and inquisitive mind concerning human behavior. Questioning my own dilemma in those days I was determined to find a method if not a cure for my failings at trying to keep a reasonably clean house.

When my first husband and I were stationed in Korea, we were able to afford a daily maid. I observed her methods and realized that she never stopped moving. I had a sister who operated the same way and her house was never messy. She was always busy, busy (I must mention that she never had kids) and she worked hard at her day job. I'm not a mover I'm a plop down on the couch sitter and agonizer when it comes to having to get up and prepare a meal. I especially loathe washing dishes and scrubbing pans. Let's face it **I HATE THE KITCHEN.**

I CAN'T CLEAN, DON'T MAKE ME!

One day back in the US while visiting my boss for whom I was doing part-time assignments I walked into her living room and it had every manner of junk littering the floor. I could see the kitchen table where cereal had been spilled, dirty dishes left, milk not returned to the fridge, and butter smeared on the counters with sticky jelly remains. She cleared a spot on the couch for us and she dropped down with an exasperated expression. She said, "I can't get caught up with my business, with these three piggies of mine." I knew what it was like to have messy "piggies." Trying to inject a little humor into the situation, I blurted out, "Why don't we just take them out in the back and shoot 'em!" She busted out laughing and we both laughed till we cried.

Another time I was so distraught from trying to get my 7 and 8-year-olds to clean their room that I threatened to take them down town to the orphanage if they didn't start picking up their toys. They both started crying and it became obvious that this was not the way to go. So, I sat down on the floor and helped them finish the job, which is what I should have done in the first place. I realize now that I missed a teaching opportunity.

I was recently talking to a good friend of mine and she told me that her mom taught them from day one to take out one toy at a time and put it back before they took out another one. They made their beds and picked up after themselves. She said it was something they just accepted as a way of life. Their mom was smart enough to take the time to teach them in the beginning, which saved her a lot of hassle in the end. She started early.

In my child rearing days, I assumed that others who were successful with holding down a day job and keeping a tidy home were both not lazy and the stay busy types. I try to remind myself of the many successes with my offspring. I emphasized affection, would not tolerate disrespect in words or actions, taught them to be kind to women, encouraged a sense of humor and put forth many many more positive messages early on. However, there were many things I left out. It never occurred to me to teach them how not to be messy. As a child I grew up in a big family and we had a maid. So, we could slob around all we wanted with impunity. We were not taught early and as we grew older we agonized over every little chore that came our way.

I CAN'T CLEAN, DON'T MAKE ME!

Of course, I really don't blame my messiness on my upbringing. I still think I am just lazy at the heart of it. I still needed to develop ways to keep a tidy home life. I was not a person who thrives on disorder. I was miserable in the mess. Over time I wanted to overcome my failings at home. Slowly I began to look at the problem differently and conquered habits that had stymied my progress in the past.

In this chapter, I mostly cover the issues of teaching children about tidiness. My past included working in a daycare center, I was a teacher's aide in elementary school, took courses in child psychology, raised two kids and fussed over my grandchildren. I've always felt I had a talent for talking to children. I wanted them to like me. So, I'm going to put forth a few ways that I have found successful with getting young kids to manage their areas.

TALKING TO CHILDREN

In the old days parents would demand that children obey or else. But if you are one of those parents who don't believe in beating your kids into submission (hopefully no one does this these days), here are some effective ways to create success even for the laziest parent.

This may sound silly but I suggest you make notes and rehearse what you are going to say. Start with one or two easy rules. Make the conversation short no more than 2 to 3 minutes. Any longer and the child's eyes will roll back in their head while they are planning their next activity as soon as the talk is over. They won't hear another word.

Here is a scenario for the first talk for most toddlers. It's best to set the rules first for their bedrooms or play rooms i.e. the children's' domain.

RULE 1

Put a laundry basket at the foot of each bed. Explain that when they take off their clothes it goes into the basket. (Do not use a centrally located hamper in the hallway or bathroom). Each kid must have their own basket so it is more apparent who is following the plan.

RULE 2

Pin the top sheet to the blankets and tell them all they have to do is pull the bed covers up to the pillows every morning. This is a very simple way to make the bed and put the jammies under the pillow. The jammies will stay clean for the next night instead of flown across the floor or kicked under the bed.

See that they repeat these two steps every day until it becomes habit. Add new steps every two weeks. Keep the steps simple. If you make the rules too complicated like: "Keep your room clean." You will find yourself echoing this refrain: "Your room is a mess, throw away those empty candy wrappers, put your toys away, and those smelly socks in the hamper and make your bed!" The result is that you will become exhausted after repeating the rant several times. The kids will be sitting in their room bewildered and accomplishing little. Each time they are scolded they will be internalizing resentment and frustration. Eventually you will despair as this scenario becomes a vicious cycle.

If the kids' bedroom is a disaster the next steps may require some pre-cleaning by the parent/s and the child/ren.

Remove cups, plates, food- stuffs, gum or candy wrappers and broken toys or other odd items before introducing the next steps. This step works best if the room starts off tidy. It's easier to keep a room clean than it is to clean a disaster. You don't want to scare off the little ones before they even start.

RULE 3

Throw all the toys into one big bin for now. These will need to be organized at a later date. Yes, I said organize, a dirty word in the "lazy, I don't want to clean" mindset. After putting toys in the bin, this is the new rule: Only one toy out at a time and to be put back before bringing out another one. This will mean that lazy parent will have to leave the couch occasionally (best time is during commercials) to enforce the rule repeatedly in the beginning until it becomes habit.

RULE 4

Coloring books, crayons, reading books, papers, markers, pens and pencils and even scissors and glue should be put into another bin to be organized at a later date. Use of these items should not be out together with a toy and should be returned to box after use. Obviously, parent must check periodically.

Rule 3 and 4 will take longer to habitualize but time is on our side. No hurry, the kids are ageing slowly when you start early.

The rest of this book will offer more simple rules which apply to everyone in the family. It will speak to the very messy teens and embarrassed adults who want change but are too overwhelmed and feeling paralyzed by their situation.

Read on, I guarantee the methods start easy and go in steps that barely challenge the laziest homemaker.

Chapter 2
Before You Start

I DON'T CONSIDER this book a massive undertaking. I have purposely kept it to as few pages as possible to emphasize the simplicity of its scope and its message. If you want to achieve your best possible results by making this endeavor a little more manageable, I have a few suggestions:

DON'T START NEW PROJECTS

Avoid starting a new book or an intensive project. Postpone a vacation or upcoming family visits. Don't put in too much extra overtime at your day job. This home project will definitely enhance future projects and boost many other aspects of your life, but first you have to commit to a small

amount of time and energy to this endeavor. You will not be disappointed with the results. I promise!

NO NEW PETS FOR A WHILE

Training a new puppy or kitty will simply complicate the process. Introducing a new pet into the home before you instill basic patterns of responsibility into your children's lives will make things far harder too. Don't walk before you can run.

Feel free to make room for your new pet once you've accomplished most of the principles in this book.

IF YOU LOVE YOUR PET...

It is not healthy for a pet to live in a filthy home. If you already have a pet in your house that is contributing to the problem, chances are if your home is neglected, then so is your pet. Pets suffer terribly from lack of attention. No one should have a pet if they don't have the time or energy to properly care for them. If you love your pet then your affection for the animal should act as greater motivation to conquer your messy habits.

I CAN'T CLEAN, DON'T MAKE ME!

STARTING A DIET

I don't see why putting off a diet should be necessary. Actually, the two objectives might go hand in hand. They are both about commitment to improve your life, and involve a fair amount of dedication. This, of course, is up to you.

ON YOUR MARK

Make sure you have thought this out and feel this is the right time to start. If you're fully committed from day one, there will be a greater chance of success.

GET SET

Have you put off all possible interferences? Are you ready to start the process?

GO!!

Strike up the band, we are on our way!!

Chapter 3
My Promise to You:
Real Success

IF YOU ACCOMPLISH ALL, or even only few, of the exercises in this book I promise it will relieve a great burden on your psyche, and significantly reduce your stress levels. You will begin to realize that messy house equals messy life. The gloom will begin to lighten and so will your mood and self-worth. You will see things in a different way and apply what you've learned to other aspects of your life. A tidy home creates a happier atmosphere.

YOU WILL FEEL MORE RELAXED AT NIGHT AND SLEEP BETTER

There will be fewer things to worry about, fewer things to keep you up at night. It will affect your family in positive ways and provide a less contentious environment for the entire household. If you succeed in most of the steps outlined in the book you will probably lose weight, gain sleep, and be generally happier and healthier.

WHEN YOUR ENVIRONMENT IMPROVES, YOU IMPROVE

You will care more about your hair and general grooming. These pieces seem to fit together when your surroundings improve. You will gain a better sense of self-worth, and self-respect when it comes to your appearance. Be prepared to feel a whole lot better about yourself.

YOUR SOCIAL LIFE BECOMES MORE ENJOYABLE

You and your family will begin to interact more with visitors. The kids will love entertaining their friends. You won't panic as much if your mother-in-law drops by unannounced, in fact you might even open the door instead of pretending no one is home!

WELCOME THE PETS

If you've been waiting to have a new pet in the household, it might be a great time to get a new puppy, kitty or guinea pig. Remember to make the rules and habitualize them. No time to get sloppy now.

TAKE YOUR VACATION

If you've been putting off a much-needed vacation, this might be a good time to take it. Remember if you slob back into your old ways during the vacay, be sure to tip the maid who cleans the room every day. Then go back home and resume your good habits.

START THAT NEW PROJECT

Have you always wanted to paint in your free time? Been dying to read the great new book everyone is talking about? Have a desire to pick up yoga? The time for you is now! All this time you've been putting off everything you actually want to do is over. Once you have set up a steady cleaning routine, it won't dominate your life, and will rarely leave you flopping onto the couch in a funk anymore.

By now "cleaning" is much less intimidating and you have the time and the drive to do the things you love.

YOUR FUTURE

Sounds exciting doesn't it? Some of you may be thinking, "This doesn't apply to me because I'm single and I don't have a family."

If you are single, messy and lazy you will still benefit by reading this book. It will help to direct your future habits before they get stamped into your brain. You will actually have a head start over those who already have families, as you will know exactly what to do in preparation for if and when you start your own. Get it right the first time. You don't have to convince anyone but yourself!

Whoever you are and whatever your circumstance, your life is about to change for the better by following these simple actions.

I CAN'T CLEAN, DON'T MAKE ME!

Chapter 4
Playing the Piano

WHEN LEARNING to play a tune on the piano on
can start with a few bars, and play them over a fe
times until it commits to memory, before moving on to mor
of the song. You have the option to go at your own speec
You don't need to put much pressure on yourself. You ca
parse the song into manageable sized pieces, and work you
way through at your pleasure.

This is exactly how this program works. Easy does it; go a
your own pace; master the first aspect before you go on t
the next. I have designed this method so that each and ever
little result will give you a huge boost as it comes in sma
manageable   doses.   You   will   feel   excited   t

go on to the next phase, like completing levels in a game. It will become less like a list of tasks, and more like a fun puzzle to complete.

Of course, if you've had piano lessons in the past and ended up hating it, then imagine an instrument that would be more fun to play, say the ukulele, guitar or a harp. Your choice! Remember that most of the anguish of housecleaning is in your head.

Suppose you had to climb a mountain in 8 hours. It would be exhausting and I know I would stop after an hour and slide back down to the bottom and cry. But if we only had to climb a small section each day, it would be manageable and we would eventually all make it to the summit. Housecleaning, when it becomes a huge task is like taking two steps forward and three steps back. It keeps getting dirty faster than you can clean. Cleaning isn't a mountain to be tackled all in one go.

I have read and researched so many books and articles with multiple tips on housekeeping. Few actually mention dirty, filthy homes of folks who have individual issues that make it almost impossible to follow the majority of the instructions. Most books tell you how to clean but most of us know how to do it. Scrub this, scrub that. Wipe these, dust those. The theory of cleaning has not always seemed simple. They tell you which products to use, the best way to make your bed, and the proper way to coordinate colors for example.

It's wonderful to be able to do all the things suggested in the "cleaning how-to books." But many of us have to "clean" before we can "clean." This book will essentially grease the wheels, paving the way for you to follow the advice offered in those books, a prequel if you will. I am about to explain why we aren't there yet.

I call myself lazy, and certainly there are a lot of us out there. There are also thousands, if not millions, of homemakers who have disabilities, mental or physical, chronic pain or depression and a hundred other conditions that make traditional types of "cleaning" unrealistic. These folks need methods that come in small and achievable packages, which they can build upon at their own pace. I promise each bit in itself is guaranteed to make an immediate difference.

It needs to be restated that this program is not for hoarders. Hoarding is a medical condition that requires guidance from trained psychologists. If you are unable or unwilling to throw things away then this is not the book for you. Discarding items is at the heart of mastering the ability to make and keep a tidy environment. Remember, this is not a hurry-up and do it all at once kind of exercise, only to stop while it builds up again.

We are about to take the baby steps that will relieve us of the seemingly overbearing task of cleaning. No need to "hold-on" as it will be smooth sailing from here on. Guaranteed.

Chapter 5
Scariest Room
in the House

I HATE THE KITCHEN, I've always hated the kitchen. I spend as little time in there as humanly possible. It is a revolting place that can never stay clean. Cleaning the kitchen is pure drudgery. Dirty plates, glasses, cups, knives and forks, pots and pans swirl in my nightmares! Sticky counters, crumbs of all kinds, and oven grime! How can this not push many of us into endless procrastination? It's enough to make you never want to cook again, which is why lazy folks often eat-out or order-in.

I CAN'T CLEAN, DON'T MAKE ME!

You can never have too much pizza? No! That's why many of us put on weight.

Is there any way out of this dilemma? I have few neat little tips that will make cleaning the kitchen more tolerable. If your kitchen is a disaster right now, I suggest you pluck up the energy and clean it the old fashion way. Maybe you can enlist the help of a good friend, or family member, or just hire some outside help.

KEEPING THE KITCHEN CLEAN WITH A LOT LESS EFFORT - GO PAPER

Use paper plates, bowls, and cups

Using paper products reduces the number of times you need to use the electricity and hot water of a dishwasher

Washing dishes by hand can use up to 27 gallons of water per load

Using an older model before 2013 dishwasher can use slightly less

Newer dishwasher models use much less

Tree farms exist to help replenish paper products, water is much more dear

Paper products can be used in the microwave

I CAN'T CLEAN, DON'T MAKE ME!

Paper products do not leave the same eco footprint as discarded dishes and pot and pans
Simply toss the dirty items in the trash

Since my husband and I went paper, we only use the dishwasher every 7-10 days. A full family has to use the dishwasher almost every day. Using paper will reduce that almost by half. Your time in the kitchen will also be reduced. No stacked-up dirty plates, bowls or standing glasses. I still use my coffee cup and quickly rinse it for the next morning. Everyone else follows suit.

So, what about pots and pans you ask? Big meals mean big messes. Keep it simple. Plan your meals so you only need to use one pot or fry pan (large or small depending on the contents). I suggest buying the new copper pots that food does not stick to. A quick swish and it's clean! Use baking bags on a cookie sheet in the oven. You will seldom have to clean it. I line the bottom of the oven with aluminum foil to catch any drips that get away.

Veggies can be heated or steamed in the microwave. Use ready-made salads that come in bags, or buy mixed greens that have already been triple washed (no cutting boards need apply). Put salad in individual paper bowls if you like.

Even potatoes can be baked in the microwave or oven. No mess there! Precut fruit saves time chopping and leaves your knives for meat and other things.

REFRIGERATOR

I never buy more that I think will be used in 1-2 weeks. Don't stuff your fridge with too much food that can go bad, and eventually smell. Always store leftovers in plastic bags. That way you throw it out when the contents get green and furry. Who wants to rinse out a plastic container with smelly rotten food?

I put kitchen towels in the fridge drawers to soak up any leaks that happen occasionally. Just change out the towels periodically and no scrubbing is needed.

I CAN'T CLEAN, DON'T MAKE ME!

TABLE AND COUNTERS

Keep a container of cleaning wipes nearby and swab all surfaces (dining table, countertops and breakfast bar) straight after a meal. It will sanitize the kitchen, and won't give the food time to dry against the surfaces. DO NOT use sponges as they are essentially petri dishes for some pretty nasty bacteria. The wipes will disinfect any raw meat juices that may have escaped their packages. These juices can be the start of salmonella, or worse. Cleaning wipes can also be used to quickly swipe the faucets, toaster, coffee maker and refrigerator in less than 30 seconds. Quick and easy.

UNLESS YOU EAT OUT BREAKFAST, LUNCH AND DINNER, THE KITCHEN CANNOT BE AVOIDED

If the message here sounds a little "much" to you, sit down, take a deep breath and reread this chapter. You will realize that the alternative is not a user-friendly option. The kitchen simply cannot be ignored. If the notion of using paper products is offensive to you in some manner, consider it a temporary fix and develop your own variation.

GROCERY LIST

I include this information as an option. Making a grocer list is an additional way to reduce the chaos in the kitchen an is something I use religiously. It can be done in the comfo of your own easy chair and help save money by stopping th shopper from picking up items you don't need. I created a lis of all the grocery items we use and categorized ther according to similar foodstuffs and dry goods. Included in th list are non-food stuffs that we usually purchase at th grocery store. A sample of this list is found on the next page.

I CAN'T CLEAN, DON'T MAKE ME!

SHOPPING LIST

BATH
Toothpaste
Deodorant
Shampoo
Conditioner
Hand soap
AC filter
PRODUCE
Avocados
Sweet potatos
Tomatoes
Cucumbers
Onions
Spinach
Potatoes
Carrots
Oranges
Grapes
Watermelon
Acorn squash
Peppers
Lemons
Mushrooms
Apples
Strawberries
Celery
Fruit
Mixed greens
Veggie platter
Salads
Bananas
SNACKS
Popsicle
Chips
Sodas
Kid's Candy
Chocolate
Cashews

FROZEN
Brussel spts
Corn dogs
Peas
Carrots
Corn
Broccoli
Spinach
Pizza
BAKERY
Cookies
Cereal
Tortillas
Taco shells
Bread
Peanut butter
Hot dog buns
Hmbrg buns
OTHER
Honey
Sugar
Brown Sugar
Taco Sauce
Honey BBQ
Decaf Tea
Coffee
Jelly
Lemon Juice
Lime Juice
Pan Spray
Parmesan
Pistachios
Coconut oil
Baking Soda
Cornstarch
CAN/JAR
BBQ sauce
Applesauce

Mayonnaise
Broth
Black olives
Ketchup
Mustard
Baked beans
Green beans
Salad dress
Soup
Tom sauce
Chili
Bread/butter
Pickles
Cranb sauce
Steak sauce
Pineapple
MEAT
Steak
Chicken
Sausage
Turkey Dogs
Turkey Breast
Hamburger
Pork Chops
DELI
Lunch meat
Chicken Salad
Potato salad
DAIRY
Milk
Heavy cream
Eggs
Butter
Swiss cheese
Cheeses
Shred cheese
Sour cream
Cottage chse

Blue cheese
Pmnto chse
DRIED
Spaghetti
Wild rice
Crackers
PPR/PLAS
Baggies
Trash bags
Paper plates
Napkins
Baking bags
Toilet paper
Facial Tissue
Paper towels
Paper cups
Paper bowls
Printer paper
CLEAN
Cleansers
Comet
Glass cleaner
Bleach
Laundry Det
Dryer sheets
DW soap
Dishcloths
Dish soap
MISC
Cat food
Cat snacks
Cat treats
Cat litter
Newspaper
Printer ink

You can even set up a regular online delivery service from your local supermarket, that way you avoid any impulse buys while trawling the aisles, and it will save you another weekly job.

Managing the kitchen has been a stumbling block for me all my life but since I created the simple routine I have outlined in this chapter, I'm never nervous about someone dropping by for an unannounced visit. The kitchen at its worst may be "in progress," but there will never be days' worth of dirty dishes, pots and pans piled up all over the place. People will say, "but you should clean up as you go along."

We, the lazy ones, are not most people and sometimes we just need to sloth out on the couch. Don't overwork yourself. Unless you love cooking and cleaning up after dinner, those cleaning minutes still count and add to the time you spend in the kitchen.

Because this step-saving routine is so easy, cleaning up after a meal is a breeze. I can even delay the task if I have an important call or another immediate issue. Going back to the

I CAN'T CLEAN, DON'T MAKE ME!

job is no longer intimidating because it will literally take only 5 to 15 minutes to finish up.

Chapter 6
Follow the Yellow
Brick Road

IMAGINE YOUR USUAL entrance to your home as the beginning of a path I like to call the yellow brick road. It is filled with different sections and stops along the way to the "emerald city." The emerald city is a euphemism for where we want to end up.

When everyone enters the home, do shoes, jackets, keys, purses, books and backpacks get shed and thrown all over the place? If the answer is yes then this is probably the first and

I CAN'T CLEAN, DON'T MAKE ME!

most important line of defense to stopping the mess before i gets started.

ACQUIRE CONTAINERS

If you have a coat closet nearby that isn't stuffed witl junk, by all means start by asking everyone to kick their shoe off and toss jackets and coats in there. If there isn't one the put a container near the door for shoes. If you are broke start with cardboard boxes or plastic laundry baskets. If yo can afford something more stylish, buy nice wicker baskets or an equivalent alternative.

Now you need to put a table or designate a surface nea (maybe unfold a card table temporarily) to drop book: purses, mittens, backpacks and other miscellaneous item: Add other smaller separate containers for keys, mail an possibly newspapers and magazines.

There is always going to be a chaos of items near th entrance and exit to your home, what you need to do i control and organize this madness.

ANOTHER WAY

Instead of too many containers at the entrance, inform everyone to walk all their stuff back to their bedrooms. Include instructions detailed in the coming chapters: nothing on the floor, nothing on the beds.

HOOKS OR HAT RACK

If no coat closet is available, install some hooks or use a hat rack to accommodate jackets or coats.

THE EVIDENCE

If you follow the above instructions, even if you go no further, the difference in your home will be astonishing. Some may say it's not very attractive to have boxes or containers around the entrance, but just remember, some of these fixes are temporary and can be tweaked at a later date. For now, this is the beginning of your personal yellow brick road.

Imagine what the front room will look like in just one day of this practice. In fact, when discussing the new project with the family, ask them for just one day to see how it works out.

It should provide enough evidence to get them on board. If not, it will probably be the teens who rise up with the most objections. Tell them that you pay for the cell phones and you can stop at any time.

After a while, they will come to appreciate how much easier it is to find items in a rush when they're stored away in an organized fashion.

I CAN'T CLEAN, DON'T MAKE ME!

Chapter 7
Papers

AS WE STEPPED on to the yellow brick road we need to address all those paper bits of mail, homework, and bills we bring into the house with us. As you look around do you notice them floating all over the place? Have you experienced the frustrating aspect of trying to find the important items later?

These items are going to require another container, which should be put in a convenient place of your choice. It will hold ALL important papers listed below, for example, and other stuff not mentioned.

1) Mail

2) Bills

3) Report cards

4) Receipts

5) Letters

6) Important Notices

7) Paycheck vouchers

8) Checks of any sort

9) Bank statements

10) Homework

This will be your "holding area" to be triaged, dealt wit
and filed at a later time. The goal of this exercise is to restric
papers from being scattered all over the coffee tables, kitche
table, counters and various other furniture surfaces until the
finally get dealt with. If you are trying to find something
guess what? If it isn't filed away, it will be in the box.

The beauty of having a table near the entrance, container
to store various items, and a central location for papers is tha
it removes the stress of looking for the keys, or asking "wher

did I put my purse." Of course, we never get tired of saying "What did you do with your homework?"

Designate a final location for newspapers and magazines until it's time to throw them out.

Determine a spot where you pay your bills, make calls and do your daily business activities. Keep your temporary paper container at arm's length where you can sort through important documents. This may be a "given" to some folks but I have memories of trying to pay a bill and not being able to find the checkbook, a pen, stamp or envelope. Relieve yourself of this chaos and keep all the necessary office items in one place.

Lastly, throw stuff out often! You wouldn't think this would need pointing out, but many times I would find my "box" full of empty torn envelopes and endless grocery receipts to name but a few lingering items.

So, up to this point we've made a fair amount of progress. We've stopped a lot of mess right at the entrance to the home by employing some quick and easy storage techniques.

In the next chapter we are going to discuss what happens when we venture from the couch.

Chapter 8
Getting off the Couch

"**W**HAT? WHY? I HATE getting off the couch!" A response to which I can relate.

TIMES WE VOLUNTARILY LEAVE THE COUCH

1) To pee
2) To get a drink
3) To get a snack
4) To get a book or magazine
5) To adjust the thermostat
6) To get a pen or pencil

I CAN'T CLEAN, DON'T MAKE ME!

7) To settle a debate between the kids

8) To make breakfast, lunch or dinner

9) To feed the dog or cat

10) To change clothes

11) To take an aspirin or a pill

12) To take out the trash

13) To turn on some music

14) To let the dog out

15) To sew a button or remedy any number of situations

I venture to say that there are at least 15 or so reasons we arise from our position of relaxation. Each time is an opportunity to quickly grab something off the coffee table or floor and throw it away or put it back where it belongs. Train yourself to NEVER get up without doing this. The goal is to clear surfaces of things that don't belong there, and to generally tidy up rubbish. You must demand family participation in this effort. In fact, you must demand their cooperation in all these steps, assuming everyone agreed at the outset (with threat of cell phone confiscation).

I CAN'T CLEAN, DON'T MAKE ME!

PROCRASTINATION IS OUR BIGGEST ENEMY

The reason we plant ourselves in the easy chair is that we are putting off the big chores we dread. What if we chop up all the big chores into little bitty ones?

Let's say we are procrastinating by watching a really great show on TV. If you are watching Network TV there will be umpteen commercials to accomplish small tasks.

DURING THE COMMERCIAL BREAKS

1) Put a load in the wash

2) Fold some clean laundry

3) Load the dishwasher

4) Vacuum half the living room

5) Clean the cat box

6) Pull stuff out of the dryer

7) Empty the trash

8) Dust the furniture

9) Change the sheets

10) Toss out dated or old stuff from fridge

11) Wash a pan

12) Ask a child to pick up a toy

13) Remove any soda cans

Of course, these days we record many shows or watc
movies without commercial advertisements. So, in this case
suggest promising yourself to do at least three things befor
you sit down. Ask this of your family members as well befor
they light up the Internet. For a family of four, that works ou
as twelve chores already!

Keeping things off the coffee table and furniture: Ever
time you get up from the couch, take something with you. I
you are going to the kitchen take something that belong
there. Do the same if you are going to the bedroom. Pick u
a sock and throw it in the hamper.

THE LITTLE THINGS WILL EVENTUALL STACK UP TO MAKE A TIDY HOME.

It's most productive to pick up like items such as cups an
glasses, all clothing items, and all trash items, for example. I
you have toddlers it is likely that you have multiple little toy
around. Keep a container to toss toys in as they increase i
number during the day. Stop accumulation in its' tracks.

I CAN'T CLEAN, DON'T MAKE ME!

These are just a few of my favorite tips for cutting the big jobs into little ones and it's even more effective when everyone does it at the same time. Invite the hubby to participate. Double, triple or quadruple the end results!

This is the philosophy of KISS. Keeping it simple, stupid.

In the next chapter, I recommend some new rules and special reminders to keep us on track during this time of transition.

Chapter 9
Rules and Keeping
Things off the Floor

I USED TO SAY, "I should have raised goats, at least they would eat the junk off the floor."

To be honest, I didn't really let my house stay messy for days on end. I couldn't stand it. I would eventually muster up the energy every few days to scoop up all the litter and make the place somewhat presentable. But I really needed to use shortcuts to make it less of an ordeal.

If you haven't had a family meeting yet now is the time to have one. If you have had one, you need another one now

I CAN'T CLEAN, DON'T MAKE ME!

TIME TO SET THE RULES

If you can't swing a dead cat without hitting clutter lying around that doesn't belong, then you need to remind your folks that a new lifestyle plan is underway!

Have you ever gone into a friend's or families' bathroom and seen everything from towels, underwear, and other clothes lying across the floor? That's a big no no. Explain to everyone that you are going to initially post a sign that says "NOTHING ON THE FLOOR," as a reminder. You know how the signs in public bathrooms say, "Please wash your hands before leaving." They post those signs because it actually works. Seeing something in black and white registers in your brain to actually modify your behavior.

You can put the signs in the bedrooms along with a gentle reminder now and then to read the signs. It will reduce the amount of screaming you had to do before the changes. If you're worried about these signs looking unsightly in your home, use them as an initial starting point, to be removed once everyone has gotten the hang of it.

Consider using hooks to hang up those things that often find their way onto the floor.

TODDLERS AND TOYS

Good luck with this one. Don't get me wrong, there are actually some toddlers who will put toys away of their own accord. They teach this in daycares after all. But then there are the little ones who will protest, scream, and throw a full-throttled fit. In this case you will probably have to do most of the picking-up yourself for a while. Again, keep a container in the living area and one in the bedroom and just toss the toys in there.

Some will say "Aren't all those containers going to be unsightly?" Maybe, but not as unsightly as your living room becoming a junk yard.

So, every time you emerge from the couch to pee or get a snack, pick up a rattle and drop it in the box. Gather up the small pieces first so you don't end up stepping on them later.

ADDICTED TO YOUR PHONE OR COMPUTER?

We are going to progress bit by bit. If things are getting out of hand because you can't pull your head out of your phone, do the following. Pick a time in the future that you are going to "start" a full task. Say, 10AM. Use the alarm on your

71

phone or just regularly check the clock. At 10AM, take a 5 o 10-minute block of time to begin your chore. After the period head back to the couch and climb into your phone.

See that wasn't so bad, was it? Blocks of time frames a easier than attacking a whole mountain of mess at once. Tric your mind into accepting a short task. You might actually g over the time limit you set without even noticing the extr time it took. Yet, even staying within a 5-minute limit you wi be surprised at how much can be done in just that snippet o time.

MAKING LISTS IN YOUR SPARE TIME

In the comfort of your own chair you can make a list o jobs you would like to accomplish over the coming hour days or weeks. Refer to the list in chapter 8 for ideas. Don feel pressured to do them all at once. As you finish each on cross it from the list. The feeling of crossing off a chore like lifting one more pound off your back. It gives you feeling of accomplishment, and drives you on to complete th next one. Get the kids involved too, if possible. Let each on choose their own task, spouse also. It's mood altering! After a while, get them to create their own lists for their bedrooms.

ROMANCING THE BIG PROJECTS

There will always be the big projects. There's no avoiding it. Not every job can be chunked down into small and manageable 5-minute increments. Whatever the big job is, do it to music if it helps your mood. If everyone has been mostly following the rules, the job will probably fly by faster than you'd think.

You should only need half a day or less. Use a list, and let everyone choose a chore starting with the youngest able one of the group. When all is done let that be its own reward. I've learned over the years that bribes, stars and candy don't work, and can also set a bad precedent. These are chores your family should be doing, not favors to you.

TEENS

Some teens are our punishment for all the bad things we've done in life.

When it comes to cleaning, teens are able but unwilling.

When negotiating with these irrational young humans, talk don't shout, at least in the beginning. Have a short meeting explaining what you are trying to achieve. Let them know that you already realize they will always come up with something they have to do instead of cleaning. Point out the beauty of picking up after themselves, there will be less to clean later. Ask them to plan ahead and be available once a week for a half day or less for pitching in. When all else fails remind them who pays for the cell phones and the Wi-Fi. Once you have given them the details of the changes about to take place, the only thing left to do is PRAY!

Chapter 10
Motivators and
Panic Motivators

CERTAIN THINGS motivate us to clean a messy house. Even the laziest homemaker can be moved to run around the house to the tune of the "Flight of the Bumble Bee" as my husband calls it.

A MODERATE MOTIVATOR

Perhaps an air-conditioning repair man is coming to check the thermostat.

We might get up and push a few things around. Drape the dirty dishes in the sink with a kitchen towel. We will

I CAN'T CLEAN, DON'T MAKE ME!

close the bedroom doors and hope he doesn't need to use the bathroom. We might even clear the kitchen table.

A GREATER MOTIVATOR

If you are expecting a good friend or family member, you might pick up the front room, wash the dishes and do a quick wipe around the bathroom, closing all the bedroom doors.

PANIC MOTIVATOR

If the Queen or your mother-in-law is dropping by, it's time to put on "The Flight of the Bumble Bee" and haul ass.

Pick up any junk in the living areas, vacuum, dust and throw things in the closet. Make beds and kick things under them. Throw bigger things in the closets and close the door. Wash dishes or put them in the oven. Wipe down counter and mop the floor. Spit shine the bathroom and spray some smelly stuff. Keep all bedroom doors open, you don't want her to think you are trying to hide anything.

If your adrenaline is in top shape, I figure you have accomplished all this in less than an hour! Of course, this an unpleasant prospect, and we would like to avoid this situation which might result in heart palpitations or worse.

But desperate times call for desperate measures.

Chapter 11
Knick-Knack No-Nos

DO YOU HAVE a large number of knick-knack loitering around multiple surfaces, waiting years to be dusted or positioned back upright? This is a common problem for messy homemakers. The trinkets that once seemed cool and nostalgic are essentially littering the household. People who keep a neat and tidy home love to display their shiny ornaments. For those of us who normally don't have a neat and tidy home, knick knacks make a messy home look messier.

Pick a few favorites to keep out and store the rest until you have shiny clean surfaces to display them. The fewer the

I CAN'T CLEAN, DON'T MAKE ME!

better with less dusting of multiple objects. In doing thi
though, you still must remember to dust the few knick-knack
you leave out. They can be fun to look at, but not whe
they're covered in dust and grime.

Hang small picture frames instead of placing them uprigh
on coffee or end tables and other surfaces. Get used to
keeping those surfaces clear of non-essential items. Item
hanging, or fixed onto the wall take up less space and gathe
less dust. It is a worthy goal to not have random items lyin
around contributing to a cluttered appearance. Adding clutte
to the home is adding chaos to your life, and we could all us
a little less chaos.

If you have a piece of something that you aren'
particularly fond of, THROW IT OUT. If it was given to yo
by a favorite Auntie, then put it away and bring it out agai
just before her next visit.

If you have indoor plants that aren't thriving particularl
well, put them outside. Too many vases with dusty fak
flowers? OUT!

OTHER ITEMS TO CONSIDER

1) Put all books in shelves, except the one you're reading at the time

2) Extra clocks, you only need one in each room

3) Videos go in one container

4) Notepads, keep just one out

5) Scissors, tape dispensers and paper clips go in a handy drawer

6) Combs, brushes and hair ties really?

7) Hammers, nails, pliers etc. go in tool box

These are just a few of the things I find lying around and promptly put them in their place. I trained myself and you can too. Again, pace yourself, any improvement over time is a win!

ATTEMPT TO CONTROL SPENDING HABITS

Before you buy, think to yourself, do I really want this? Do I really NEED this? Is it a useless and decorative item that will only add to the stuff that just gets knocked around and eventually tossed out? Especially be aware of BOGO Two useless items are worse than one.

As we move along there are still a few large tasks yet conquer.

Chapter 12
Laundry, the Lazy Way

I LIED, THERE IS NO lazy way to do laundry, but there are many ways to reduce the amount of work and make it less mind-numbingly painful to complete.

The following suggestions highlight some amazing ways to make washing day more tolerable.

STOP WASHING SO OFTEN

Install hooks in the bathrooms to hang towels so they can be reused instead of ending up on the damp floor. Damp towels on the floor will often have to be washed immediately.

I CAN'T CLEAN, DON'T MAKE ME!

creating more work for yourself. You can use the heavy-duty stick-up hooks if you don't want to screw them into the wall. Also, over-the-door hooks can be added for bathrobes or additional towels.

Note that original towel racks are awkward and end up holding bunched-up tips of towels later to fall down.

USE A LAUNDRY SORTER

If you don't have one, get one, or at least use 3 separate laundry baskets in the laundry room. One for dark, light and colored items. I know, more baskets, but it's easier than stepping on piles of mixed clothes, or mixing that one red sock into your white wash.

KEEPING STUFF OFF THE FLOOR

Sound familiar? One of the most important aspects to reducing wash loads is finding ways to keep things cleaner longer.

Keeping pajamas under the pillow saves them from the floor, and ultimately, the wash sooner. Pinning sheets to the cover or comforter helps keep the sheet from slipping to the floor and ending up dirty.

Make sure clean clothes go directly from laundry room to drawers. I've seen this a million times. Kids and sometimes adults will put the fresh washed clothes on the bed and leave them there until bedtime. They get pushed aside and end up on the floor, sometimes getting mixed up with the dirty stuff.

Train yourselves and your kids to stop this vicious cycle.

HATE FOLDING CLOTHES?

Try folding clothes while watching a TV program. Have each person put away their own clothes IN DRAWERS not on the bed. This way everyone has a sense of responsibility for their own stuff, as well as knowing exactly where it all is when they need it. Now is a good time to use the option of a sign "Clean Clothes Go in the Dresser Not on the Bed."

There is no need to fold underwear or socks. In fact, I learned to buy only white socks for my family to avoid all the mismatches. They go in the wash with the white clothes and bleach, which actually helps reduce "stinky feet socks."(Soon after I adopted this practice of using all white socks, the

department stores got wind of it and now it is very hard t
find a pack of all white ones).You might even be able to wea
them twice. Let's say a family of five wears white socks ever
day. That equals at least 5 pairs a day for a week. Fifty sock
What if sometimes the socks were worn twice? You cou
reduce the wash-load by as much as twenty socks! If yo
enjoy your multicolored socks, you can always put them in
mesh bags to keep them together.

Another tip for storing clothes is to hang more. Invest
some plastic or wooden hangers and use them for anythir
"hangable." This includes dress shirts, dresses, trousers,
shirts and jackets. This saves loads of time folding.

Also, if some clothes need to be ironed for work, th
ironing will be much easier if the item was hung right out o
the dryer. Often clothes actually won't need much of an iro
if you hang dry them neatly.

Search wikiHow's articles on how to fold faster. There a
some clever moves to hasten the job.

This folding method can also be found in the "wikiHow'
articles, but I first encountered it in Korea. I was packing fo
a trip and my maid showed me a clever way to fold clothe

I CAN'T CLEAN, DON'T MAKE ME!

She folded most everything first in half and then rolled it like a tube and placed each item next to each other. Doing it this way actually saves more room in drawers and suitcases. You can even roll up multiple items together when packing into a tight space. There are tutorials online showing people how to pack a t-shirt, pair of trousers, pants and socks all together in one tube. It leaves the clothes almost wrinkle-free! You have probably seen this done with towels in chic home-style magazines. We did this with our towels in our bathroom when staging our home for sale. I really liked the effect. Rolling your towels takes about half the time of folding, and arguably looks nicer anyway.

Lastly, there are some new and creative ways to dress for work. Search "The Uniform Challenge." Suppose you have a favorite blouse or shirt that you feel comfortable in and it flatters your build. Match that with your favorite bottoms, pants, dress, whatever. Purchase the identical items times several days of the week. You will have created your own "uniform." No more staring into the closet agonizing about what to wear or what fits or matches. I love this idea!

ACTUALLY, THERE IS AN EASIER WAY TO GET THE LAUNDRY DONE!

This idea is almost too good to be true. I wish I'd thought of it years ago when I had teens and the wash was enormous. Hire a teen to come in once a week to do a few loads, fold and put away the items. Show them where the towels, sheets and personal clothes go. Pick a specific time for your laundry person to arrive. Have one load already washed and another load in the dryer. They can fold items from the dryer after transferring wet clothes, then put a new load in the washer. After two hours they will have finished 5 or 6 loads, folded and put away. What you pay them will be far less than a professional service.

Moving from laundry room to the bathroom. We are making progress in the next chapter.

I CAN'T CLEAN, DON'T MAKE ME!

Chapter 13
Bathroom Blues

WET TOWELS, UNDERWEAR, shoes, toilet paper bars of soap and toys lying around the bathroom floor? Toothpaste smeared around the sink? Hair ties barrettes, and bobby pins scattered about? Lipstick, fals eyelashes, and contact lens cases? Mildew appearing in th hard to reach spots around your shower? Is there a smell Yuck!

There is nothing more demotivating than a dirt bathroom. After all, the bathroom is where you come to ge yourself clean, and to get off to a good start of your day.

Below are things you need in the bathroom to prepare fo the transformation and erase the bathroom blue:

I CAN'T CLEAN, DON'T MAKE ME!

1) Hang your "Nothing on the floor" sign

2) Install hooks and racks for hanging items.

3) Keep a hamper in the bathroom to toss dirty cloth⟨ and towels.

4) Keep a small trash receptacle near toilet.

5) Keep Bubble Bath near tub,

6) Keep cleaning wipes next to toilet.

7) Keep cleanser and toilet brush near commode.

8) Keep deodorizing spray on counter.

9) Use rugs specifically made to surround the toilet.

In a previous chapter I discussed the psychological effe⟨ of having a sign as a reminder to everyone that nothir belongs on the floor. The hooks, the hamper and the tra⟨ container provide a place to toss all the possible items that ⟨ end up there.

A small amount of bubble bath in the water will prevent build-up of scum and tub ring.

A used towel is a great way to take 15 seconds to wipe ⟨ spilled water or soap.

I CAN'T CLEAN, DON'T MAKE ME!

I have been known to wipe around the commode while sitting there, which is why I keep wipes nearby. About once a week, sprinkle cleanser in the bowl and use the toilet brush to swish it around for a total of 15 – 20 seconds. Not a huge period of time to commit to keeping a clean bathroom.

Use a couple of small containers on the counter to put items that otherwise might be lying around the sink. For example, a cup or holder for your toothbrushes. A dish for your soap. A hamper for your towels.

Take a minute to teach the kids how to express toothpaste sparingly from the tube without smearing it around the sink. Also take the used hand towel to wipe the sink then toss it in the hamper.

All these tips will make your bathroom look and smell good for those periods between deep cleaning days.

Chapter 14
The Joy of the Purge

IF YOU'VE FOLLOWED along this far and implemented some, or most, of the practices outlined in previous chapters, this part can lift even further weight off your shoulders. As you unburden yourself of the mess and clutter, your mood will improve as you begin to feel more in control of your life and home.

I CAN'T CLEAN, DON'T MAKE ME!

TOSS IT OUT

Here are some items to consider getting rid of in the toy bins:

1) Broken toys
2) Puzzle pieces
3) Dried up markers and pens
4) Broken crayons
5) Torn color books
6) Naked Barbies
7) Scratched CDs and DVDs
8) Other items unredeemable

KITCHEN TOSS

Get rid of any uneaten leftovers in the fridge. Out dated food items should always be discarded before they smell, which also frees up space for other items. During the purge of the fridge it is a good time to wipe down the shelves and wipe off any sticky residue on ketchup bottles or jelly jars before returning them to the fridge. Below is a list of many other kitchen items to toss:

1) Broken or chipped dishes
2) Cracked cups or glasses

3) Outdated cereal boxes

4) Outdated foodstuffs

5) Bent or broken pans

6) Badly tarnished dinnerware

7) Outdated spices

8) Tupperware tops and pieces

9) Any indoor plants you have killed

BATHROOM TOSS

There is a lot of stuff in the bathroom that you may not realize needs to go:

1) Expired prescription medicines

2) Outdated over-the-counter medicines and vitamins

3) Old toothpaste

4) Old toothbrushes

5) Remnants of bars of soap

6) Old cosmetic items

7) Old shampoos, conditioners and hairsprays

DONATE

Here are some items in good shape to donate that you ma
no longer need:

1) Toys
2) Clothes
3) Shoes
4) Games
5) Books
6) DVDs
7) CDs

You can also donate old blankets and towels to anim
shelters. Goodwill, as of now, will also take old TV's ar
computers. In most cases you can call your Was
Management Co. or trash collector to do a special pick-up f
old furniture and large appliances.

I have probably left out a few things but you get th
general idea. This process should take less than a day. So, pi
a day in the future and invite a friend or family member wh
would be willing to help. Put on some great music and rewa

yourselves with some wine and cheese when it's all said and done!

Chapter 15
Everything Has a Place

FIRST CREATE a common location for the majority o
'things,' whether you use them frequently or not. All
can say is, in time you're going to pay. If you don't believe m
I direct you to Chapter Sixteen, Disasters of Our Ow
Making.

Common locations can consist of everything from empt
bowls to baskets placed in agreed-upon places, or a hand
drawer or cabinet. This concept cannot only contribute to
neat home, but can go a long way to maintaining peace o

I CAN'T CLEAN, DON'T MAKE ME!

mind by reducing the chaos of searching for those damn ca[
keys! Few things can start a shouting match faster than th[
following.

"Who's got the remote?"

"You had it last!"

"Well it didn't grow legs and walk out of here!"

"You need to put it back where it belongs!"

"Where does it belong?"

Here is a list of a few items that could use a common agreed[
upon location:

1) Remote

2) Car keys

3) Scissors

4) Cellophane tape

5) A purse

6) Reading glasses

7) Pencil or Pen

8) Cell phone

9) Nail clippers

10) Calculator

11) Screwdriver

12) Aspirin

13) Stapler

14) Flashlight

I CAN'T CLEAN, DON'T MAKE ME!

I could go on forever naming items that are easily misplaced. Whenever my husband asks where something is, I can easily tell him where to find it instead of where to get off. It's because while walking around the house if I see something lying around I pick it up and put it in its designated place. I avoid shouting matches for petty reasons.

Chapter 16
Disasters of Our Own Making

THE FOLLOWING stories are true, and are the resu of laziness, not putting things where they belong, lac of attention to details, animal mishaps, toddlers getting in things, not teaching your children proper use of applianc and other related occurrences.

CROCKPOT RICE?

Years ago, when my kids were young, I made a love dinner in the Crockpot.

I CAN'T CLEAN, DON'T MAKE ME!

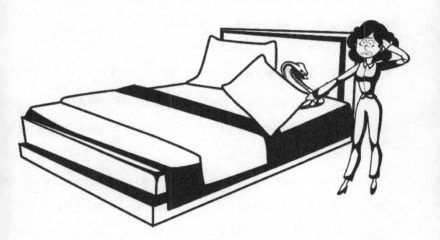

While cleaning up I must have been distracted and forgot the Crockpot. I don't know how many days passed before I noticed some rice near the lid. After lifting the lid, the rice seemed to be moving. Aaagh!! Maggots!! I quickly bagged the whole pot and lid then threw it outside in the trash. I bleached the whole kitchen. I didn't cook with a slow cooker for years after that horrific experience.

ORANGE YOU SORRY WE DID THAT?

Trying to get my little ones to clean their room was always a challenge. I remember one particular event that was a little more stressful than others.

They were fooling around, as usual, and getting nothing done. I finally caved-in, sat them down and told them each thing they had to do. I spotted half an orange lying face down on the dresser. I picked it up and saw that several bugs had been setting up housekeeping on the slimy surface. Yuck! I showed it to the boys and they responded with "eeww!"

It wasn't long before that lesson was wasted on them.

Instill a sense of responsibility and routine from an early age to avoid these mishaps.

I CAN'T CLEAN, DON'T MAKE ME!

ANOTHER ORANGE STORY

My brother in his pre-adolescent days loved to eat oranges. He would ensconce himself on the couch and consume his favorite snack in front of the T.V. It was probably anywhere from one month to who knows how long before someone moved the furniture to clean. Who knew that a mountain of orange peelings in various stages of decay were waiting to be discovered behind that couch. We checked behind the furniture more often after that.

A CLOTHES CALL

Later on, my same brother and I were sharing a home while attending the same university. He hadn't matured much in his messy ways. His routine consisted of shedding his clothing where he stood. There was barely a clear spot on the bedroom floor. One morning he told me about a crazy dream (nightmare?) he had the night before. Apparently, he had some kind of sleep paralysis and was struggling to wake up as his clothes had arisen from the floor and were attacking him in his bed. We had a good laugh. Think of the irony!

SLIP SLIDING AWAY

I remember one time I took my two granddaughters to th
movies. I let them pick their snacks at the concession stanc
with one of the girls getting her favorite snack befor
hopping off to the butter dispenser. She loved lots of butte
on her popcorn. We watched the movie while she happil
munched on her popcorn. After the feature was over, we gc
up to leave. I noticed her lap was soaked in butter, which ha
obviously leaked through the container. Then I saw a shin
floor under her feet. It was slick with butter! The older gi
went to get lots of napkins. People were gawking as I wa
profoundly embarrassed trying to desperately wipe up th
mess. I could have left it for the staff, but I was afrai
someone would slip and really hurt themselves in the dark.
did the best I could and told the ushers what had happene
as I left the theatre with a sorry look on my face.

A SURPRISE FOR THE CAR MECHANIC

A family member, who I won't name, had an absolut
obsession with Taco Bell. She would drive up and order
couple of tacos quite frequently, and after finishing her mea

she would crunch up the wrappers and stuff them in various nooks and crevices within the car. This went on for some time until she had to take the car to the mechanic for an engine repair. She was called to come and pick up her car a day later. When she got in the car to go home she noticed that all the wrappers from Taco Bell had been removed. She was burning with shame as she drove out. It was never mentioned on subsequent car repair days, but she stopped stuffing wrappers in the car.

You should always set aside 10 minutes every month or so to clean out the rubbish from your vehicle.

FIRE IN THE HOLE!

When I was 15 I was taking care of my siblings one morning while my parents were gone for a while. We had a shoot from which to toss dirty clothes from the top floor to the laundry room on the bottom floor. There was a gas water heater with a flame underneath. As we threw our clothes down the shoot they began to build up due to some procrastination on our part to do the wash. Apparently, the last person to walk out of the laundry room accidently kicked

a piece of clothing toward the flame. It wasn't long befo
one of my sisters raced up to tell me there was a fi
downstairs. I quickly filled a pan of water and flew down
the laundry room. but by then the flames were too high.
threw the pan in, closed the door and got everyone out. Th
entire top floor was torched. As we stood outside with th
fire trucks I saw my Dad pulling up in his truck. He had
sick look on his face as he was counting heads. All us ki
and the animals were unharmed. When the house was rebu
the laundry room was reconfigured with many safe
measures.

It just goes to show that laziness and procrastination ca
have some dire consequences.

MOUSE IN THE HOUSE

We were stationed in Korea living in a high-rise apartme
on the top floor at the time. We had a maid who had her ow
quarters just off the kitchen. She was great, took good care
the kids and kept the house sparkling clean. One day
noticed some suspicious looking coffee grounds on the stov
I didn't really think it could be mouse droppings as we we

on the twelfth floor, but I put a piece of cheese on the stove that night. I checked it in the morning and, sure enough, the cheese was gone. I still wasn't convinced it could be a mouse though. That night the mouse was struttin' his stuff from the kitchen to the front room, and made direct eye contact with me on the couch. He had attitude and refused to move until I flew into a rage and stomped and screamed, at which point he finally scurried off.

The moral of this story is as soon as you are sure you have a mouse infestation, take care of it immediately. I quickly put an end to that smart-ass rodent and his smart-ass kin.

THE CATS' FIRST MISTAKE

Of the two cats I got for my sons, one turned out to be less of a bundle of joy than the other. Being lazy, I left my bed unmade until after breakfast. I went back in once I'd finished eating and pulled up the blankets and covered the pillows. The cat that had been sitting on the bed left the room due to my disturbance. That night I crawled in between the sheets and stuck my foot down into something wet and squishy. I threw the covers back to see this disgusting deposit of poo on my pristine white sheets. Instead of being able to climb back into my comfy warm bed I was now forced to strip the bed and wash the soiled area. After about 30 minutes delayed slumber, I found it difficult get back to sleep while cursing the new cat.

From then on, I made my bed immediately when arising.

THE CATS' LAST MISTAKE

The new cat must have had a 'thing' for my bed. A couple of weeks after the first incident, I walked into my room and the bed was made but on my pillow was a mouse head and another undefined mouse part. A gift, I've been told. I didn' give a flip whether it was a "gift" or not. I gifted her right back to the animal shelter. I just couldn't handle it.

Don't take on a pet if you're not ready to deal with responsibility of a mischief-maker.

TAR BABIES

We were renting a home that had a big back yard and a storage unit, which at first glance appeared to be empty of all contents. That would soon be proved wrong in a very unfortunate circumstance. My two young ones, and a playmate, discovered a can of tar up in the so-called empty storeroom. They progressed to paint the back porch, side of the house, retaining wall and eventually for extra fun each other. Their playmate started wailing and I went out to see what all the commotion was about. He was upset that his mom might be mad because he had accidentally tarred his new watch. I knew this outcome wouldn't end well, especially when his stocky German mom gave me a piece of her mind, along with some nasty expletives.

I asked a friend for help and we spread a blanket down on the floor in the front room. We stripped the boys and laid them down. We chose several remedies to get the stuff out of their hair, eyebrows, hands, feet, arms and legs. It was a near impossible undertaking for a couple of hours while they squirmed and whimpered. We used Vaseline, alcohol, polish remover and dish soap. We were unable to remove all of it and one final bath made little difference. We had to let it wear off over the next few weeks. Thank God it was the summer. If they had to attend school I probably would have had a visit from Social Services.

Always keep an eye on your little ones, and keep dangerous items well out of reach, especially when they have friends over.

CREATIVE CRIMES OF KIDS

Case and point with this next story.

The minds of 4 and 5-year-olds are full to the brim of never-ending chains of machinations. One day I was expecting some friends to visit, and as I was greeting them the male guest went into the kitchen to make himself a drink. Apparently, I hadn't put the bleach back where it belonged. My friend called out to me and I came in to see the broiler open with an active flame and two very guilty looking youngsters standing by. He told me that they were in the process of pouring bleach into the broiler pan. I was shocked and it seemed inconceivable to me that they could dream up such a scheme. I asked both of them what were they thinking. The older one tried to blend into the woodwork as the 4 year-old huffed and puffed and sputtered out an answer, "I don't know mom, sometimes we get these crazy ideas."

I CAN'T CLEAN, DON'T MAKE ME!

DISHWASHER DISASTER

The following story is the reason I didn't require much cleaning help from my teens. I don't know if they screwed things up on purpose so they didn't get asked again, or if they were just that stupid. I told my 15-year-old to clean up after fixing his own dinner. He dutifully put the dishes in the dishwasher, and started it. A while later my kitchen was overrun with bubbles and soapy water. I thought the dishwasher was broken and called for maintenance. It turned out my genius teenager had added washing up liquid instead of dishwasher powder to the receptacle.

Never assume they know what to do, give them clear instructions and supervise for the first time doing any chore.

SNAKE IN THE BED

Always avoid leaving the sliding doors open. Once you've read this next story, I won't need to explain why…

I was lying on my pillow with my two toddler granddaughters, and asked my daughter-in-law to bring me a naper for the little one. As she was bringing it to me I sat up to change the baby, at which point the 3-year-old jumped

away from me screaming "there's an animal under th
pillow!"

Her mom pulled the pillow away that I had been leanir
on just a few seconds earlier. To our shock and horror, it w
a curled up black snake. The little girl screamed, "It's stickir
its tongue out!"

My daughter-in-law went screaming for my son as we
evacuated the bedroom. My son came flying in with a was
can and I yelled, "Don't let him disappear, I'll never be ab
to sleep in this room again." He finally collected the snal
into the can and returned it to the backyard.

TAKING A STAB AT IT

I saved the best for last. I doubt few people have ev
experienced this tribulation but it could happen if you are la
about putting things back where they belong.

I was at my mom's house and she was sitting and enjoyir
her 3-year-old grandson's company. My two-year-old and h
cousin were sitting on the couch when I came bounding ov
to give them a cuddle. As I landed on the couch, I levitated
nanosecond later leading with my pelvis. It must have been

ilarious sight to my mom and my son as even she was trying to stifle a hysterical laugh. I was seeing stars and feeling nauseous as I looked down to see that I had plopped my butt down precisely upon a pair of scissors, with blades sticking up between the couch cushions. Everyone continued the hilarity as I went to assess the puncture wound in my behind.

From snakes to scissors, these are true stories of my life. My point was not only to provide a lesson or two but to remind us to not take ourselves too seriously.

Chapter 17
Housekeeper
Wanted

YOU NEED TO BE RICH to have one follow you around day and night. They provide a great service when it comes to providing you with a clean slate so to speak. But you might be surprised to know that a good housekeeper can get a lot done in just two hours.

So why did my family have one daily? Because we had six bedrooms, three bathrooms, an eat-in kitchen, living room, family room and a recreational room. Big house, big mess and she did all the washing and ironing. Poor woman, but my dad paid her well.

DIXIE LEE JOHNSON

I was not rich, a single parent with an average income. Some folks with big houses can't pay the house cleaning rate these days, but most of us can afford a couple of hours help once in a while to get us back on track.

As I mentioned in a previous chapter, for some there is the option of asking a good friend, neighbor or relative to give you a hand or trade something in exchange for their help. You might have people close to you who don't mind seeing you at your worst.

Most of the time I did some pre-cleaning before they arrived. There is always an element of "personal dirt" nobody needs to see. Maids have told me war stories where they would enter a home with a weeks' worth of dishes in the sink and an army of flies between them and the job.

As with anything in life, some of us are in worse shape than others. I learned of a recent widower who had no clue how to function in the kitchen or how to run a dishwasher. His occasional housekeeper was an angel who understood.

My favorite scheme is the one of hiring a teen to do your laundry for a couple of hours a week. It won't break the bank and will take a load off your shoulders. They can wash your eets and remake the beds. What a dream! Some of the ziest homemakers might put off washing day until they are rced to make their kids wear a pair of underwear for a cond day in a row.

When you do let someone into your home here's a word the wise. I had someone in to clean my apartment once but had to go to work before they were done. My roommate ld me later when she came in she saw the maid sitting on e couch eating a sandwich and watching TV with her feet 1 the coffee table. She wasn't getting much done. But it uld have been worse it's best to stick around while the aid is working, or at least set up some kind of nanny-cam.

Chapter 18
Organized Mess

U P TO THIS POINT we have concentrated on what w
call organized mess. On the surface the house real
doesn't look messy. However, the floors probably nee
mopping or vacuuming, tubs and toilets need scrubbing ar
the house needs dusting.

It is not necessary to attack all these items in one day. Pi
one and put it behind you. If your home is reasonably tid
these chores will not seem overbearing, and won't take up to
much of your time.

Like most of us, I would read a book like this through
the end before I actually put it into practice. Then I would

mull it over in my head for a few days. If I felt it was a plan I could follow I would go back to the beginning and start the project. Once you have accomplished most of the steps and have established a nice rhythm, you might be ready for further action.

TRUE ORGANIZATION

Organizing is a wonderful thing. It is mood lifting. I love it. I pick a time in the future and an area that needs organizing then jump straight in. It can actually be very therapeutic.

There are literally hundreds of books and articles on the subject. They call them "hacks" on the internet, and so many are clever and very inspiring. Go to the web and enter something like "hacks for organizing your home."

If you want to go beyond articles on the Internet take a look at my list of recommended reading at the end of this book.

I CAN'T CLEAN, DON'T MAKE ME!

Chapter 19
Prevention

HERE ARE SOME alternate tips and prevention techniques to stop trouble before it starts. Some of you may have started with cardboard boxes or plastic laundry baskets at the home entrance as part of your "yellow brick road" back in Chapter Six. Or, you may have purchased some less tacky and fancier hampers.

Train everyone, including your spouse, to walk their stuff back to the bedrooms. Leave some designated places up front for keys, mail, purses and other things that could be otherwise misplaced. Remember maintaining clear space enhances the appearance of a tidy home.

If you have a nice couch and like to eat there in front of the TV, throw a sheet over the furniture and toss it in the laundry when it gets dirty. Replace it with another while the original is in the wash. If company is expected just yank it off until they leave. You will have nice clean furniture to impress your guests.

I will mention it again because this is one of my favorite prevention techniques. Put hand towels in the bottom of refrigerator drawers to catch sticky drips from fruits and vegetables. All you have to do is replace them with clean ones every so often, with no scrubbing needed.

Use a container to hold all your spices. Pull out the container when you need access to one, and then remember to put them all back neatly.

It's very handy to just put the microwave plate in the dishwasher.

Keep little paper cups to gargle with or swish mouth wash. They are sanitary and can be dropped straight into the waste basket.

I CAN'T CLEAN, DON'T MAKE ME!

Use foil to line the bottom of the oven. You can also wrap the drip pans with foil under the burners to avoid sticky stains and burn marks.

Use an old rug to place under the cat litter box to minimize scatter. Also, a small rug under the pet dish and water dish will absorb drips and bits.

Stuff extra plastic grocery bags in the bottom of waste cans to simplify disposal.

I hope these extra tips, many of which you may have been already aware, help to make cleaning a little less difficult in your home.

Chapter 20
Consider Green

I HAVE MANY RESERVATIONS about recommending plastic in this book. Most people these days are becoming far more aware of the miles of plastic Styrofoam and other waste floating in the oceans. Fish have been ingesting more and more of this garbage, with plastic straws being a major contributor.

A lot of restaurants now offer paper straws, to cut back on this threat. One of the worst offenses today is using plastic six-pack holders. They cause all kinds of trouble for sea creatures. I would avoid buying products that use those, or at least cut them to bits before throwing them away.

I CAN'T CLEAN, DON'T MAKE ME!

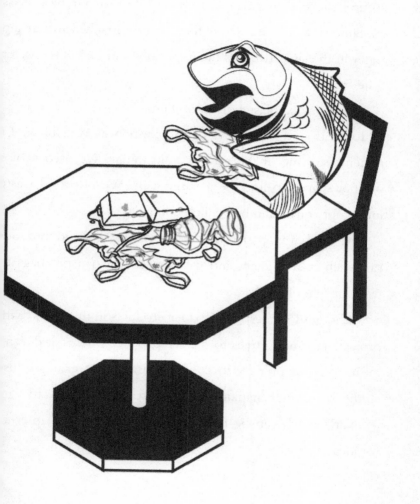

Plastic water bottle waste can be linked and stretche around the planet a couple of times. Try to purchase glas containers. We have a water filter device attached to our ta water in the sink. It filters the impurities and makes the wate taste fresh.

Avoid buying plastic drink containers.

I was around in the days before plastic was available and remember some of the ways we did things. We used to us old newspaper to line the garbage cans. We put food wast into empty quart and half gallon containers.

We used wax paper bags to store food or to put ou sandwich in for lunch, and we carried brown paper bags t work or school.

Although I suggest using paper products in this book, wit projects replanting trees to replace paper resources, it doesn mean we shouldn't try to conserve usage. For example, us cloth for dinner napkins. There are many ways to "g greener" which can be found simply by asking the Interne for ideas.

I CAN'T CLEAN, DON'T MAKE ME!

Chapter 21
In a Perfect World

NORMALLY, WHEN WE READ a self-help book w
get all excited in the beginning and can't wait to sta
employing the new ideas. Unfortunately, after a while the ne
ideas lose their appeal, excitement fades, and in no time, w
slide back into our old habits.

My sister recently asked me: how do you make a hab
stick?

In her experience, every time she tries a new regim
whether it be a diet, a workout schedule, or a way of life pla
she eventually fails at the attempt. The beauty of this proje
is that you can always drop it at any time. Eventually,

I CAN'T CLEAN, DON'T MAKE ME!

believe, when you get tired of the mess around your home, you will pick it up again. It will always be in your head. Just like the sign that says, "Wash your hands" in public bathrooms, it will stick with you.

Remember you don't have to adopt every suggestion in this book. Maybe you hate eating off of paper plates. Planning your meals to be one pot cooking, or using a baking bag with your meat and veggies cuts down on the number of pots and pans. Ponder ways to make meal preparation simpler. Maybe you can buy pre-prepared salads with included salad dressings. Have each person wash their own plate, dinnerware and glass (wash, dry and put away in cupboard). If they don't like the washing part they can be the one eating off the paper plate.

As I said before, you can modify the yellow brick road by having everyone walk their stuff straight to their rooms. Yet keep the keys, mail and messy boots in a consistent place near the entrance. The best way to get this to stick is to remind everyone repeatedly until you don't need to any longer. Think of what a difference this simple change will make.

I CAN'T CLEAN, DON'T MAKE ME!

Maybe you can pay one of your kids instead of a stranger to do 2 hours of washing, drying and putting away laundry. Don't expect them to do it without compensation. They will miss the opportunity of learning how to earn a wage. You will also be normalizing the process of cleaning for them, making it less of a shock when they eventually get their own place.

Once you get the idea in your head about taking something with you when you get up from the couch, that idea and routine will stay with you. It will ultimately manifest into an automatic action, like muscle memory. Believe me! That is exactly what happened with me.

As you look at your coffee cup sitting on the coffee table, you may have stepped past it four or five times without picking it up (as I often do). That sixth time might be the time you actually do it. The idea will never leave your mind. As you realize that the one coffee cup will become the one sock, and then the one toy, then the one coke can (you get the point) and they get ignored before long it becomes a big job to clean up. Once the one thing becomes the fifteen things and the pile continues to grow, we sink into procrastination mode as we avoid the inevitable disaster.

Then we're back where we started. When an area is clear single item will stand out on its own. You may ignore it bu once it becomes two or three items you will realize that th three items can quickly multiply into fifteen. Hopefully, yo will snatch them up before they proliferate.

Those are the kind of thoughts we are going to have whe looking at that one coffee cup.

If you have a family you can say "would you please tak that magazine with you and put it in the rack?"

The same can be said to the husband or to the toddle who is no longer playing with a specific toy. YOU must b the instigator for a while until it becomes a habit with certai members of the family. You will find they will quickly do just to avoid the resultant nagging.

Imagine (in your mind) starting a small task or the firs step of a large task. Just thinking about the deed ca sometimes precipitate an action.

When you live with others, you can always delegate. As said before, ask nicely and they might actually do it.

I CAN'T CLEAN, DON'T MAKE ME!

DONATE

key to keeping a tidy and organized home, is to get rid of so much extra stuff. There are many needy people out there who could use some of those jackets you no longer use. Consider donating stuff that is piling up in the garage or store room. Listed below are some items which may no longer be useful to you and are taking up space in your home:

1) Old clothes
2) Shoes
3) Extra crock pots
4) Dishes
5) Furniture
6) DVDs
7) Flatware
8) Old toys
9) Coffee mugs
10) Duplicate glasses
11) Small appliances
12) Duplicate tools
13) Excess Christmas decorations
14) Towels
15) Linen
16) Books
17) Blankets

Make getting rid of things something you do periodically. This may not become an established habit but after you have done it once, you may become motivated again at a later date.

DIXIE LEE JOHNSON

I recommend an article: "How to form a new habit (in easy steps)." By S.J.Scott, writer of many books abou forming habits. I hope I have given you some new perspective on how to establish a thought process that wi encourage a new approach to accomplishing your routin housekeeping habits.

I CAN'T CLEAN, DON'T MAKE ME!

Chapter 22
Conclusion

AND THERE WE HAVE IT, that concludes my little book of tips for the lazy, challenged or handicapped homemaker. I hope that at least a few of the ideas and stories in this self-help tale have resonated with you and inspired you to make a difference in your home.

Remember, any big job can be split down in to far more manageable increments. You never have to take on more than you can manage, and completing these minuscule tasks on a daily basis can actually be the secret to maintaining a clean and healthy home.

Now that you have reached the end of the book, go back through the contents and circle or highlight the

I CAN'T CLEAN, DON'T MAKE ME!

chapters you want to focus on first. Start small, work your way up, piece by piece. Once you get the ball rolling, get your family involved, and make small cleaning chores part of your routine, the house will take care of itself.

It's amazing what a clean and tidy home can do for the mood and the soul. Living in dirty areas can often spread to your psyche too. Clean house, clean mind.

Not only this, but teaching your children the tips in this book will set them up perfectly for life, and will minimize the risk of them falling into the same bad habits that you have. Be the one to make the change. Start the chain. Teach the lessons that will be taught to your grandchildren, and their children, and their children after them. If we don't have robot cleaners by then, that is.

I would like to leave you with this one final idea:

I wish I could travel back in time and give this book to myself then. I can only wonder what a difference it would have made in my life.

Here's to a happy and healthy home!

RECOMMENDED READING

Jhung, Paula. How to Avoid Housework: New York: Simon & Shuster

Includes in depth cleaning techniques for each room in t house.

Talks about starting the toddlers early in their housekeepi habits.

Discussions of starting them early. "You go into a nurse school and you'll see two-and three-year-olds pouring their ov juice, making their own peanut butter sandwiches, and picking their toys," said Dr. La Corte. "Yet we expect so little of them home."

Nursery school director Carol Doughty agrees. "We teach t children to be self-sufficient here in the classroom, but as soor Mom arrives, they become helpless again."

She discusses killer clutter."Clutter can be hazardous to yo mental and physical health. It has caused fights, divorce, anxie alienation, injury and even death."

Concerning toys she states:"Hide and rotate toys a few at time. Interest cools with too many, and pickup is tim consuming.

More about clutter and furnishings: "Don't confuse Hou Beautiful with House Clutterful. Those country cottages choc full of collections may look cozy but they demand consta care."

Jhung, Paula. Cleaning and the Meaning of Life: Deerfield Beach, Florida: Health Communications, Inc

Based on decluttering your home, arranging your closets, bill paying, shopping and how it impacts your life
Jhung suggests inviting a houseguest. The procrastinator's guide to letting go:
I dare you to call your mother-in-law. See how fast you straighten up then. I bet even the laziest of us will at least move a few things around (haha).

Bredenberg, Jeff. How to Cheat at Cleaning: Newtown, CT: Taunton Press

Discusses clutter control, laundry, sanitation , your car, your yard and all the main areas of your home. I like what Jeff Bredenberg says. He's not your mother and he's not looking over your shoulder. "Your mental health is more important than being a slave to someone else's ideas."
Bredenberg says a 30minute TV show will have about 8 to 12 minutes of commercial ads; recommends a Roomba@ or one of its competitors, however if you are reading this book I wager it won't get 2ft before running into something that doesn't belong on the floor.

Harris, Cerentha. Feather Your Nest: New York: Marlowe and Company

A guide to cleaning your house, controlling bacteria, storage and having a place to put everything. She recommends having a place for everything and investing in plastic containers.

ABOUT THE AUTHOR

Dixie Lee Johnson is from Colorado Springs, Colorado. She spent 10 years in the US Army while raising two boys and was the first female to give birth to two children while on active duty. She trained in X-ray technology then Ultrasound during her service. Ms. Johnson continued in the field of medical Ultrasound

after leaving the military. She has lived in Korea and Saudi Arabia and traveled around the world visiting many countries.

She graduated from the University of Colorado with a B.A. in psychology and acquired multiple medical registries during her life. She now resides in Melbourne, Florida.

Being the oldest of five siblings and three stepsiblings gave her many experiences and opportunities to observe the family dynamic from an inquisitive perspective. All of which provided groundwork for the book. She reports that she has been writing this "manuscript" in her head for many years. Now she is thrilled to put it out there for others to experience and hopefully assimilate the lessons into their own lives.

Made in the USA
Las Vegas, NV
16 August 2023